Surviving the Insanity

A Gift for a Loved One in Jail or Prison

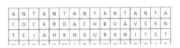

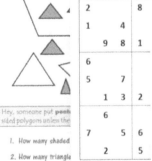

by C. Mahoney

Life is about choices...

It's NOT enough to just "survive" life and its **frustrations** and **annoyances**. You want to **EXCEL** in life, succeed, do well, **beat** the snot out of those who dare say that you can't get what you want and do what you want in life. Well, get up and do something about it. Do **MORE** than **JUST** survive.

You're in jail. Prison. And life **SUCKS**, sure. That's just the way it is right now. You're surrounded by morons. You're told what to do every day: get up, go to bed, get out of the restroom, eat, stop eating, walk here, don't walk here, go outside so we can take your stuff, stop, go, put your hands behind your back. It sucks! But what are you going to **DO** about it? Whine? Complain? Gripe to the nimrod bunked nearby? That won't do **you** any *good*.

Even though you're stuck there, **DO** something about it now. **Improve** yourself. **Read** at least one book every week. **WRITE** a letter to someone and tell them about your life there, your thoughts, your emotions, your goals, your plans, your hopes and dreams. **Work out**, every day, sculpting your body into something that you can be proud of, something strong and tough and durable. **Learn** a new language or teach someone yours. Make **choices** that are good for you, your mind, your body.

Do **MORE** than **JUST** survive each day there. **Improve** yourself.

Now turn the page and see what follows. You just might find a few things to help you along your way.

Challenge ONE

> Therefore, to him who **knows** to do **good** and does NOT do it, to him it is a **sin**.

James 4:17

Think about the words above and what they mean: having an opportunity to do something nice for another person. If you have the chance and you don't do it, then it's just like you're doing evil or meanness or rudeness to that person. Take advantage of the opportunities you have to help another guy do his time today. Play cards or chess, and win or lose, whatever, just play and laugh and smile. Loan a stranger a book so that he can fill up the empty hours of the day. Sit down and ask a guy how things are going back home with his loved ones, and listen, and be nice.

What are three good things you can do today?

1. _____
   _____

2. _____
   _____

3. _____
   _____

Did you know...

1 Did you know that there are over 9,000 kinds of grasshoppers?

2 Did you know that a grasshopper's jaws move sideways?

3 Did you know that a grasshopper has five eyes?

4 Did you know that when grasshoppers make noise by rubbing their leg against their wing they are trying to find a mate?

5 Did you know that grasshoppers breathe through little holes in their skin called "spiracles," not through their mouths?

6 Did you know that a grasshopper's ears are either on their front leg or on their abdomen?

7 Did you know that a grasshopper's skin is waterproof?

Sudoku

2			8	3		9		4
1		4		7			2	
	9	8	1		2	5	7	6
6				5		8		3
5		7		9				
	1	3	2		8	7	4	
	6				7			1
7		5	6		4		8	
	2		5			6		7

Yay! It's time for fun, that 1~2~3~4~5~6~7~8~9 game of Where does it go? and What goes here? and Ahhhhhh!

Enjoy yourself and don't let the numbers get you down.

A **word** *fitly* spoken
is like **apples** of *gold* in **settings** of *silver*.

~Proverbs 25:11

A	N	T	A	N	T	A	N	T	A	N	T	A	N	T	A
C	O	C	K	R	O	A	C	H	B	V	A	V	S	X	N
T	E	J	A	H	K	N	G	U	B	K	N	I	T	S	T
N	C	N	G	M	L	R	E	W	Q	T	Q	T	A	A	A
A	D	F	T	N	A	T	A	N	T	A	J	N	N	K	N
N	H	N	G	I	Y	L	F	E	S	R	O	H	A	L	T
T	A	L	F	G	P	A	N	T	P	T	V	O	B	M	A
J	K	T	N	A	Y	E	U	I	I	N	S	R	N	E	N
L	O	U	S	E	N	P	D	O	D	A	T	N	A	D	T
T	T	N	A	F	M	L	C	E	E	D	N	E	N	E	H
N	I	I	F	T	N	A	V	Q	R	W	F	T	T	P	T
A	U	T	Y	L	F	E	S	U	O	H	E	R	Y	I	F
N	Q	N	D	T	B	V	X	A	A	I	O	T	U	L	A
T	S	A	S	N	W	T	N	Z	S	K	P	N	E	L	N
T	O	U	W	A	N	T	N	A	D	C	L	A	K	I	T
N	M	Y	S	A	N	T	E	A	F	I	G	H	J	M	N
A	T	P	R	G	U	B	D	E	B	T	N	A	T	N	A

Find these words: cockroach, centipede, millipede, wasp, hornet, housefly, horsefly, mosquito, flea, louse, tick, stinkbug, bedbug, spider, ant

Bonus: How many ANTS can you find in this puzzle? There are lots of them, so look carefully. ____

HOW many triangles can YOU find?

The answer is **NOT** ten. Sorry. Try looking beyond the most **obvious**. Look for **overlapping** rectangles. That's right, rectangles that are placed on **TOP** of another. How many can you find? Here are four options, just to help you out. Pick the one you think is the answer and then go look on the answer page (just a few pages farther in this incredible book) and see if you were right. I hope so because this is an **EASY** one. You have four more challenges to go in this book, and they will get harder. Okay, what is the answer?

a) 11 triangles   c) 13 triangles

b) 12 triangles   d) 14 triangles

Colorful **words** that describe ME

Think about what you **do**, what people see you **doing** with your *body*, your *mouth*, your *face*, your *hands*, your *feet*. Action is what you do (not what you say).

Red

Blue

Green

Yellow

Orange

Black

White

Who am I?

_____

_____

_____

_____

_____

I am out on a trail, camera in hand and Nike Monarchs on my feet. I like it out here, away from people and their noise and problems and needs. Just me and the wildlife that is willing to endure my presence. I set my feet down softly as I walk, careful not to crunch the fallen twigs or crinkly leaves. A tree. A bush. A rabbit. Whoa! I freeze as it stares at me with one eye. It knows that I am there, and it is worried that I might be a threat, dangerous, a predator. I stand still and watch it twitch its nose. I blink, but it doesn't, not once as I stand still and click the shutter on my camera. It knows nothing about me, just what it sees. That's how life is, and how people are, making a judgment based on the outside. I stand still. It's what I must do.

Don't hang the spider!

A = (3 x 3) x (5 + 2)

B = 2 x 2 x 2 x 2

C = 7 x 2

D = (1 + 2 + 3) x (1 + 2 + 3)

E = 3 x 3 x 3

F = 3 x (2 + 2 + 2 + 2)

G = (4 + 5) x (11 - 2)

H = 7 x (2 + 2 + 2 + 2)

I = 1 + 2 + 3 + 4 + 5

J = (3 + 3 + 3) x (1 + 2 + 3)

K = 3 x 2

L = 8 x 4

M = (2 x 3) x (4 + 3)

N = 7 x 3

O = 1 + 2 + 3 + 4 + 5 + 6 + 7 + 8 + 9

P = 3 x (2 x 2)

$Q = 4^2$

R = 2 x 3 x 2 x 2 x 2

S = 2 x 2

T = (3 + 4) x (2 + 2)

U = (3 + 4) x (4 + 3)

V = 1 x 5

W = 2 x 2 x 2 x 2

$X = 5^2$

$Y = 3^2$

$Z = 5 x 2^2$

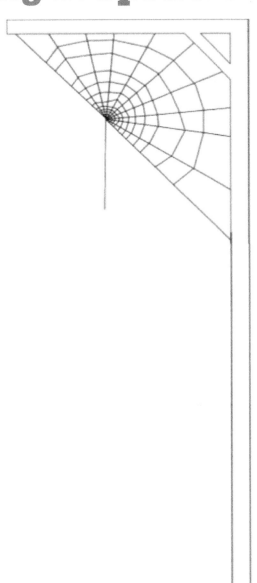

$\overline{14}$ $\overline{45}$ $\overline{21}$ $\overline{5}$ $\overline{27}$ $\overline{21}$ $\overline{15}$ $\overline{27}$ $\overline{21}$ $\overline{14}$ $\overline{27}$

If you tell the truth, you don't have to remember anything.

Mark Twain

Unscramble these WORDS

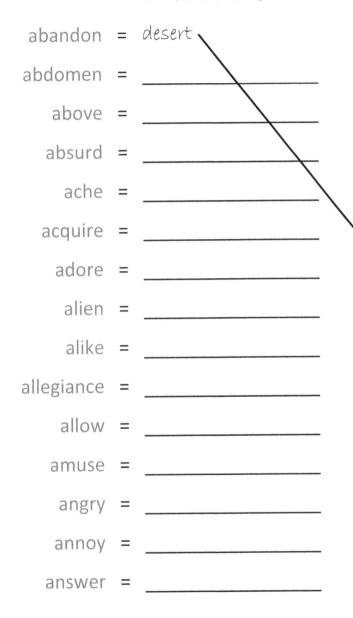

abandon = desert

abdomen = _____

above = _____

absurd = _____

ache = _____

acquire = _____

adore = _____

alien = _____

alike = _____

allegiance = _____

allow = _____

amuse = _____

angry = _____

annoy = _____

answer = _____

teg

raimisil

napi

revo

aitenertn

redest

roifegn

perly

lanioirtar

reptim

attiirre

mostcah

surufio

atyolly

vole

What am I most thankful for?

_____

_____

_____

_____

_____

_____

_____

_____

_____

_____

_____

Pick One

Circle it, write it, explain your choice. You can only pick one. No cheating! This activity gets you thinking outside the box, and maybe, outside of your cell.

 Which is more **intoxicating**, a woman in silky lingerie or the final moments before your release?

 Which is more **irritating**, another bologna sandwich or the guy who sits beside you at chow?

 Which is more **satisfying**, an hour of outside rec or a visit from your family?

 When are you more **relaxed**, when you're reading a brand new book or the moment before you fall asleep?

 Which is **faster**, your shower when the hot water doesn't work or that guy who smells your coffee and wants some for free?

 Who is **smarter**, the guy who reads a lot of books or the guy who keeps his legal problems to himself?

 Where is it more **interesting**, at the lunch tables or in the restroom in the afternoon?

Ahhhh!
It's time for us to explore the world of secret words, confusing to those who can't see beyond the letters and numbers and symbols.
But you? You're smart.
So this will be a snap.
Easy. Simple.
Enjoy the challenge.
See if anyone else can solve them...

CAN CAN

FRIFRIFRIFRI
FRIFRIFRIFRIFRIFRI

B 4

What words or phrases DO you see?

1. _____   2. _____
3. _____   4. _____

Think about it...

No act of kindness, no matter how small, is ever wasted.

-Aesop

"The hardest battle you're ever going to fight is the battle to be just you."

-Leo Buscaglia

"Memory is an abstract painting—it does not present things as they are, but rather as they feel."

-Eugenia Collier

"I'm on a journey like everyone else, with fears, doubts and challenges."

-Laura Hollick

"Death keeps it real and reminds you that every minute is precious and full of possibilities—holds that you have to reach for."

Making Words

How many *words* can *you* MAKE **from** these **letters**

A A E I O D N R R R T X Y

SHORT words 1-3 letters	MEDIUM words 4-6 letter word	LONG words 7 or more letters

What is the 13-letter word that describes you? _____

Talking about...

Imagine that a **ROCK** could TALK. What would it say? Would it be **angry** or **happy** or **silly** or try to make a **joke** or **tease** or want to **play cards** or to be **alone**?

...to the **window** it just broke

_____
_____
_____

...to the **tire** that just ran it over

_____
_____
_____

...to the **guy** who just ducked to avoid it

_____
_____
_____

...to the **bottle** that just broke

_____
_____
_____

...to the **fingers** that hold it

_____
_____
_____

Weird Facts about the United States ...

55 countries use **English** as an official language

29 use **French**

24 use **Arabic**

20 use **Spanish**

8 use **Portuguese**

Here are the **top ancestries** in the United States of America: German (15.2%), Irish (10.8%), African-American (8.8%), English (8.7%), American (7.2%), Mexican (6.5%), Italian (5.6%), Polish (3.2%), French (3%), American Indian (2.8%)

81%
of Americans
speak
only English

There are

6,912 languages

spoken in the world, but that number will decrease to about **700** by 2020.

Reasons that my life is worth living...

write a few in the spaces below

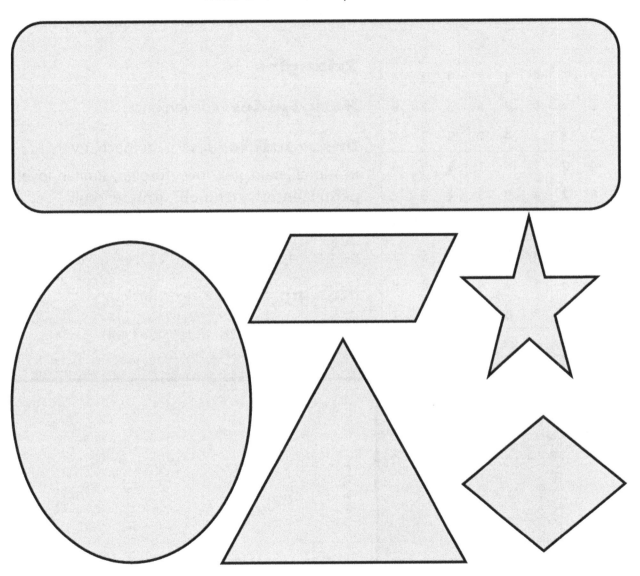

Answers

for Challenge ONE, so that you don't **freak out** wondering whether you're a **genius** or a **moron**

2	7	6	8	3	5	9	1	4
1	5	4	9	7	6	3	2	8
3	9	8	1	4	2	5	7	6
6	4	2	7	5	1	8	9	3
5	8	7	4	9	3	1	6	2
9	1	3	2	6	8	7	4	5
8	6	9	3	2	7	4	5	1
7	3	5	6	1	4	2	8	9
4	2	1	5	8	9	6	3	7

Triangles: 14

HangSpider: convenience

Unscramble: desert, stomach, over, irrational, pain, get, love, foreign, similar, loyalty, permit, entertain, furious, irritate, reply

Word Puzzlers: down to earth, toucan, frighten, before

Making Words: extraordinary

Word Search: at least 40 ants

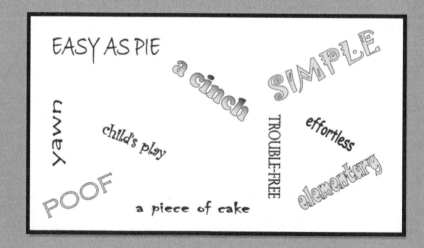

EASY AS PIE
a cinch
SIMPLE
yawn
child's play
TROUBLE-FREE
effortless
elementary
POOF
a piece of cake

Challenge TWO

> Therefore, whatever you **want** men to **do** to YOU, **do** also to **them**, for this is the Law and the Prophets.
>
> Matthew 7:12

Look around you at who you are surrounded by, men who say what is on their mind and curse and insult and threaten, guys who have lived a tough life, had to fight their way from one situation to another, stealing what they can, hitting and kicking and hurting others when the moment arose. And you. Do you like to be punched in the face? Do you like to be insulted, made fun of, talked about? No? Well, these words were spoken years ago, but they are still true today. Think about what you do in response to others, what you do to others. Think before you act.

What do you want others to do to you, here, in jail?

#1 _____
_____

2 _____
_____

3 _____
_____

Did you know...

1 Did you know that the fangs of most spiders are sideways?

2 Did you know that spiders can live for months without eating?

3 Did you know that most spiders have eight eyes?

4 Did you know that there are hundreds of tiny nozzles on each spinneret on a spider's abdomen?

5 Did you know that crab spiders can change color to match the flower they move to in just a few days?

6 Did you know that most spiders grab a fly with their fangs?

7 Did you know that the venom of a black widow is fifteen times more powerful than that of a rattlesnake?

Sudoku

2	5			6			4	
	6	1	5		8	3		2
		8	1	2			7	6
4	3				2	8	1	
		2			4			3
8	9	5	3		7	6		4
					1		6	
1	2	6	4	3				7
		4		9	6	2		1

Yay! It's time for fun, that 1-2-3-4-5-6-7-8-9 game of Where does it go? and What goes here? and Ahhhhhh!

Enjoy yourself and don't let the numbers get you down.

He who **walks** with **wise men** will be *wise*: but the *companion* of **fools** will be *destroyed.*

-Proverbs 13:20

Word Search

This collection of words is all about the LIBRARY. I know, I know. This is NOT where you spent much time.

Well, that was a choice that you made, time and time again as a youngster. Now you're an adult. Do you have any regrets? Maybe a little more focus on schooling and learning and things would've turned out differently. Maybe...

A	B	S	K	O	O	B	N	A	I	R	A	R	B	I	L
R	F	I	C	T	I	O	N	C	D	S	Q	N	W	F	D
C	H	E	C	K	O	U	T	E	T	T	R	O	E	I	V
H	I	S	P	U	Y	C	S	N	S	U	E	N	S	N	D
I	O	D	S	E	P	O	H	C	E	D	R	F	C	E	S
V	N	C	Y	L	L	M	E	Y	G	Y	U	I	I	R	J
I	O	Y	C	I	Y	P	L	C	A	K	T	C	E	E	J
S	I	H	H	B	H	U	V	L	U	Y	A	T	N	D	R
T	T	P	O	O	P	T	E	O	G	R	R	I	C	N	E
G	A	O	L	M	A	E	S	P	N	O	E	O	E	I	B
O	M	S	O	K	R	R	H	E	A	T	T	N	U	B	M
L	R	O	G	O	G	G	F	D	L	S	I	D	D	K	U
A	O	L	Y	O	O	N	O	I	G	I	L	E	R	O	N
T	F	I	A	B	E	S	Z	A	X	H	C	A	E	O	L
A	N	H	R	Y	G	O	L	O	H	T	Y	M	V	B	L
C	I	P	T	R	O	T	A	V	R	E	S	N	O	C	A
M	E	L	V	I	N	D	E	W	E	Y	M	A	T	H	C

Find these words:

archivist, art, bookbinder, bookmobile, books, call number, catalog, CDs, check out, computer, conservator, DVDs, encyclopedia, fiction, fine, geography, history, information, languages, librarian, literature, math, Melvin Dewey, mythology, non-fiction, over-due, philosophy, psychology, religion, science, shelves, study,

How many **triangles** can YOU find?

Hey, there are **shaded** triangles here. Yes. And **OVERLAPPING** triangles. And triangles all by themselves. One. Two. Three. Or something like that. Okay, here are your three questions. Think about them. Use a pencil to mark on this page, and your brain.

1. How many shaded triangles do you see? _____
2. How many triangles are completely inside another triangle (without touching any sides? _____
3. How many total triangles do you see? _____

Ten *numerical* **words** that describe *my* FAMILY

Think about your **family** and your **house**, your **car** and what you watch on **TV**, where you go for fun and the laughter and smiles and good times.

One

Two

Dozens

Millions

None

Alone

Group

My family is awesome because

_____

_____

_____

_____

_____

A rock falls down a cliff and I look at it bounce its way toward my feet. I'm alone out here, just me and my camera. What caused that? I see a movement and look up. A mountain goat stares down at me as I take photos. I wonder what he is thinking, if he is nervous about my presence or if he doesn't really care about me at all. I watch him, trying to figure it out, waiting to see if he runs in fear. He doesn't. He stands there, watching, while the females and kids walk among the trees and bushes, nibbling and eating what they want. I can't read his mind, but I can read his body, his posture, his movements, the way he holds himself erect. Confidence exudes from his stance, certainty and peace. He has no fear of me. I am not important or a threat.

Whatever...

Weird Facts about whatever...

"Men ought to know that from nothing else but the **brain** comes joys, delights, laughter, and sports, and sorrows, griefs, despondency, and lamentations. And by this, in an especial manner, we acquire <u>wisdom</u> and <u>knowledge</u>, and see and hear and know what are foul and what are fair, what are bad and what are good, what are sweet, and what are unsavory. And by the same organ we become mad and delirious, and fears and terrors assail us. All these things we endure from the brain."

-Hippocrates, 5th century B.C.

The biggest pencil, ever, was 76 feet long. It was too heavy to pick up, weighing 21,700 pounds.

The biggest book measured 26 feet tall and 16 feet wide. It had 429 pages.

Dubai
United Arab Emirates
2012

The biggest plastic duck was 82 feet tall.

France

Don't hang the spider!

$A = 4^3$

$B = 8 \times 10$

$C = 2 \times 4$

$D = (3 + 3 + 3) \times (1 + 2 + 3)$

$E = 2^3 \times 6$

$F = (1 + 2) \times (3 + 4)$

$G = 2 \times 3^2$

$H = 2 \times 5$

$I = (2 \times 3) \times (4 + 3)$

$J = 1 + 2 + 3 + 4 + 5 + 6 + 7$

$K = 2 \times 2$

$L = 7 \times 5$

$M = 1 + 2 + 3 + 4 + 5 + 6 + 7 + 8$

$N = 7 \times 8$

$O = 3 \times 8$

$P = 7 \times (1 + 2 + 3 + 4)$

$Q = 3^2$

$R = 5^2$

$S = 5 \times 6$

$T = 1 + 2 + 3 + 4 + 5$

$U = 2 \times 3$

$V = 2 \times 6$

$W = (5 + 1) \times (5 + 5)$

$X = (4 + 5) \times (11 - 2)$

$Y = 9 \times 5$

$Z = 5 \times 10$

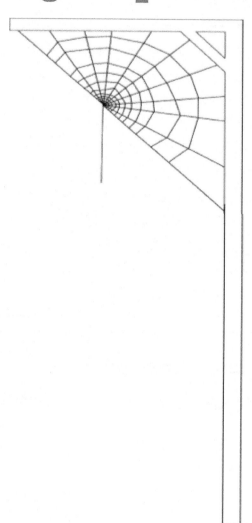

$\overline{8}$ $\overline{48}$ $\overline{36}$ $\overline{48}$ $\overline{15}$ $\overline{64}$ $\overline{25}$ $\overline{45}$

When you extend a hand, you cannot shake a fist.

– Matthieu Ricard

Unscramble these WORDS

baby = *infant*

bandit = _____

barbarian = _____

bashful = _____

bawl = _____

beast = _____

beg = _____

belief = _____

below = _____

bent = _____

bite = _____

bizarre = _____

blend = _____

blind = _____

boast = _____

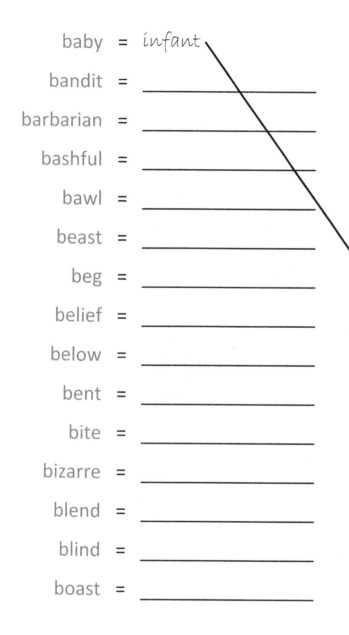

xmi

ratsgen

fithe

syh

stitewd

kas

nioniop

fanint

ewhc

ryc

garb

gevasa

gishstles

lanami

thenabe

Pick One

Circle it, write it, explain your choice. You can only pick one. No cheating! This activity gets you thinking outside the box, and maybe, outside of your cell.

 Which is **dirtier**, the mouth of an angry man or the floor beneath the toilet**?**

 Which is more **complete**, a letter that is ready to be sent home or a man who recognizes his own errors**?**

 Which is **lighter**, an empty coffee cup or the mind of a man who blames the cops**?**

 Who is **stronger**, the guy who can do burpies and squats for two hours or the man who has finished his sentence**?**

 Which is **sloppier**, the guy who doesn't make his bed in the morning or the excuses you offer to your family**?**

 Which is **sneakier**, the guy who looks in your drawer when commissary has arrived or your story about that night**?**

 Which is more **dangerous**, a lie to protect yourself or a lie to hurt someone else**?**

WORD Puzzlers

Ahhhh!
It's time for us to explore the
world of secret words,
confusing to those who can't
see beyond the letters and
numbers and symbols.
But you? You're smart.
So this will be a snap.
Easy. Simple.
Enjoy the challenge.
See if anyone else can
solve them...

sheep **WOLF**
sheep

clothing

oin**FLY**tment

SECRET

HO J U M P I N G **OPS**

What words or phrases DO you see?

1. _____

2. _____

3. _____

4. _____

Think about it...

"Nice of you to visit," he said to the empty space.

"It's always a pleasure," he answered.

He had talked to himself. Had he done that before? Well, talking to himself didn't mean anything. He wasn't crazy, he was simply lonely.

from <u>The Wager</u>

"For a long time they said we didn't need one, but then something changed and they said we did."

Pandora found hope, disguised as a butterfly, at the bottom of the box.

He heard terrified screams as he fell asleep, and he knew they were his own.

from <u>The Wager</u>

The best remedy for those who are afraid, lonely or unhappy is to go outside, somewhere where they can be quiet, alone with the heavens, nature and God... I firmly believe that nature brings solace in all troubles.

-Anne Frank

Here **is a** *blank* **page,** for **no** reason....

Making Words

How many words can you MAKE from these letters

A A E U C C L P R S T

SHORT words 1-3 letters	MEDIUM words 4-6 letter word	LONG words 7 or more letters

What is the 11-letter word that describes you? _____

Talking about...

Imagine that a **STICK** could TALK. What would it **say**? Would it be **angry** or **happy** or **silly** or try to make a **joke** or **tease** or want to **play cards** or to be **alone**?

...to the **dog** that just chased it	_____ _____ _____
...to the **shoe** that just stepped on it	_____ _____ _____
...to the **kid** who just got hit with it	_____ _____ _____
...to the **tree** that just lost it	_____ _____ _____
...to the **hiker** who just picked it up	_____ _____ _____

What *is* **most** IMPORTANT to **you?**

Make a list, here, now, on this page, inside these triangles.

Answers

for Challenge TWO, cuz it would really suck if these weren't here and you had to guess.

2	5	3	7	6	9	1	4	8
7	6	1	5	4	8	3	9	2
9	4	8	1	2	3	5	7	6
4	3	7	6	5	2	8	1	9
6	1	2	9	8	4	7	5	3
8	9	5	3	1	7	6	2	4
3	8	9	2	7	1	4	6	5
1	2	6	4	3	5	9	8	7
5	7	4	8	9	6	2	3	1

Triangles: 8 shaded triangles, 2, 22 total triangles

HangSpider: cemetery

Unscramble: infant, thief, savage, shy, cry, animal, ask, opinion, beneath, twisted, chew, strange, mix, sightless, brag

Word Puzzlers: a wolf in sheep's clothing, a fly in the ointment, jumping through hoops, top secret

Making Words: spectacular

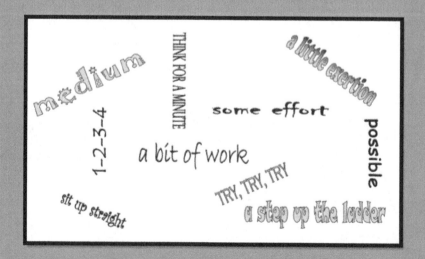

Challenge THREE

> Come now, you who say, "Today or tomorrow we will go to such and such a city, spend a year there, buy and sell, and make a profit;" whereas you do not know what will happen tomorrow. For **what is your life**? It is even a **VAPOR** that appears for a **little time** and then **vanishes away**.

James 4:13-14

Life, it is a **vapor**, a **puff** of wind, a slight **breeze** that tickles the skin for a moment and then is gone. Sure, you may live seventy years, or eighty, or ninety, if you're lucky and avoid being stabbed or shot or run over by someone in a truck. Maybe cancer won't get you, or pneumonia or diabetes. Maybe you won't have a stroke or a heart attack or just stop breathing for a long, long time. Maybe. But one day you'll be that old-timer, and you will ask "Where did all that time go?" Poof! And what will you leave behind? What great things will you have done that others see and remember and are thankful for? Think about this, today, because each moment is here and then gone.

What are two things you want to leave behind for others when you die?

Did you know...

1 Did you know that dragonflies of long ago (300,000,000 years ago) had two-foot wing spans?

2 Did you know that a dragonfly can zoom 36 m.p.h.?

3 Did you know that a dragonfly has a blind spot so hawks swoop from the rear to capture and eat them?

4 Did you know that the dragonfly is the fastest insect on earth?

5 Did you know that there are over 4,800 kinds of dragonflies?

6 Did you know that a dragonfly rests with its wings spread apart, while a damselfly rests with its wings behind and together?

7 Did you know that a dragonfly nymph lives in a pond eating other bugs for 1-5 years?

Sudoku

3	1				2	7		4
4			7				5	9
2		9		4	6	1	3	
	4			5	7	9		
	2		6		8	5		7
5		7			4		8	6
8			1				7	
1		5	4		3	8		2
	9			2	5			3

Yay! It's time for fun, that 1~2~3~4~5~6~7~8~9 game of Where does it go? and What goes here? and Ahhhhhh!

Enjoy yourself and don't let the numbers get you down.

He that covers his **sins** will **NOT** prosper: but whoever *confesses* and *forsakes* them WILL have mercy.

-Proverbs 28:13

Word Search

What do you know about the world, its people, its faiths, and its languages,? Well, hidden in this puzzle are some not so secret secrets that you might not know about. So, as you move into uncharged waters, learning about people who are not you, consider what you think and believe and know.

T	O	K	Y	O	Q	D	G	N	I	G	L	U	O	E	S
I	W	R	Q	B	O	L	U	A	P	O	A	S	F	D	E
Q	H	D	E	T	Y	W	D	S	C	I	B	A	R	A	A
K	J	R	U	S	S	I	A	N	W	R	H	U	J	N	V
E	E	S	E	N	I	H	C	N	I	R	A	D	N	A	M
D	N	P	D	S	E	L	E	G	N	A	S	O	L	E	S
Y	G	A	A	R	S	U	O	N	O	E	G	I	D	N	I
T	L	N	W	T	N	W	M	D	E	L	P	H	I	D	N
I	I	I	Q	Y	E	M	S	I	H	D	D	U	B	M	A
C	S	S	E	J	W	F	I	H	Y	L	W	I	M	S	I
O	H	H	R	N	Y	G	O	J	J	A	B	O	U	I	C
C	W	I	T	B	O	M	A	K	K	M	V	L	M	U	U
I	M	Q	N	F	R	A	T	H	E	I	S	M	B	D	F
X	I	H	U	D	K	L	D	E	Y	R	F	K	A	N	N
E	N	T	J	W	U	S	A	N	E	P	J	J	I	I	O
M	Z	X	C	Y	T	I	N	A	I	T	S	I	R	H	C

Find these **top religions** in the world: Christianity (31%), Islam (22%), Atheism (16%), Hinduism (13%), Taoism and Confucianism (6%), Buddhism (5%), Primal – Indigenous (4%)

Find these **mega cities** in the world: Tokyo (33 million), Seoul (23 m), Mexico City (22 m), New York (21 m), Mumbai (21 m), Delphi (21 m), Sao Paulo (20 m), Los Angeles (18 m)

Find these **top languages** in the world: Mandarin Chinese (1,075 million), English (514 m), Hindu (496 m), Spanish (425 m), Russian (275 m), Arabic (256 m)

How many **triangles** can YOU **find**?

Shaded triangles. **Blank** triangles. **Overlapping** triangles. You've got it now, the game, how to play. Of course. So, answer these questions:

1. How many shaded triangles do you see? ____

2. How many triangles touch another triangle? ____

3. How many triangles do NOT touch another triangle? ____

4. How many total triangles do you see? ____

Weird Facts about whatever...

In 2012, Larry Macon ran 157 marathons. Each marathon is 26.2 miles long. Whoa! That is a lot of running.

The largest hamburger, ever, had 42 pounds of tomatoes, 40 pounds of cheese, and 16 pounds of bacon.

Jacoby Jones did something pretty incredible, twice. He caught a kick off eight yards deep in the end zone and returned it for a touchdown, against the Cowboys and against the 49ers.

The largest water balloon fight, ever, had 8.957 fighters and 175,141 water balloons.

What?

Ten words that describe my CHILDHOOD

Think about what you **did**, the **games** you played, the **PLACES** you went, your friends and siblings, your parents and their friends, **fun** and **laughter** and **good** times.

1	6
2	7
3	8
4	9
5	10

My best childhood memory:

_____

_____

_____

_____

_____

_____

_____

I pass a feather and stop to take a closer look. It used to belong to a bird, a part of its coat to keep it warm and dry and alive. It used to be a part of a life, one that could fly and soar and zoom. I think of my life, what used to be, and what is now. Jail has changed things in my life, what I do, who I hang out with, where I go. It's not what it was. I no longer fly where I want. I've lost too many feathers. Now I am grounded, stuck here day after day. I try not to think about the skies I used to soar through, the freedom that I used to have. It makes me sad. Instead I think about now, today, this moment, and focus on being what I can be right now. I awoke with options in front of me, so many minutes and seconds. Though I can't soar, I can walk and run and jump.

What would you write here IF you could?
Psst! YOU can!

_____

_____

_____

_____

_____

_____

_____

_____

_____

_____

_____

Don't hang the spider!

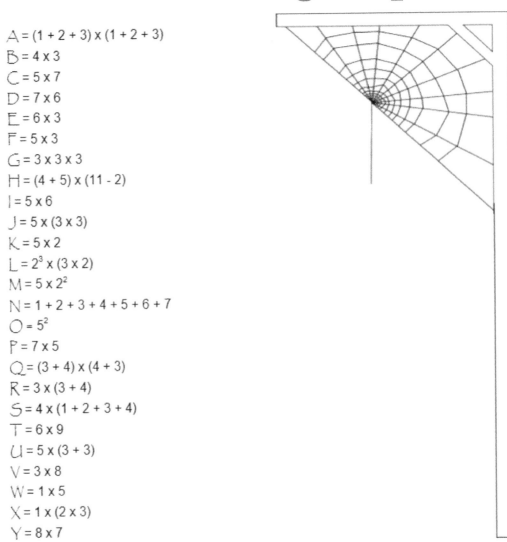

A = (1 + 2 + 3) x (1 + 2 + 3)

B = 4 x 3

C = 5 x 7

D = 7 x 6

E = 6 x 3

F = 5 x 3

G = 3 x 3 x 3

H = (4 + 5) x (11 - 2)

I = 5 x 6

J = 5 x (3 x 3)

K = 5 x 2

L = 2^3 x (3 x 2)

M = 5 x 2^2

N = 1 + 2 + 3 + 4 + 5 + 6 + 7

O = 5^2

P = 7 x 5

Q = (3 + 4) x (4 + 3)

R = 3 x (3 + 4)

S = 4 x (1 + 2 + 3 + 4)

T = 6 x 9

U = 5 x (3 + 3)

V = 3 x 8

W = 1 x 5

X = 1 x (2 x 3)

Y = 8 x 7

Z = 2 x 7

$\overline{12}$ $\overline{18}$ $\overline{35}$ $\overline{36}$ $\overline{30}$ $\overline{40}$ $\overline{18}$

The way we choose to see the world creates the world we see.

– Matthieu Ricard

Unscramble these WORDS

cab = taxi

cafeteria = _____

cap = _____

captive = _____

career = _____

careful = _____

cash = _____

cat = _____

cease = _____

champion = _____

chaos = _____

chart = _____

cheap = _____

cheat = _____

childish = _____

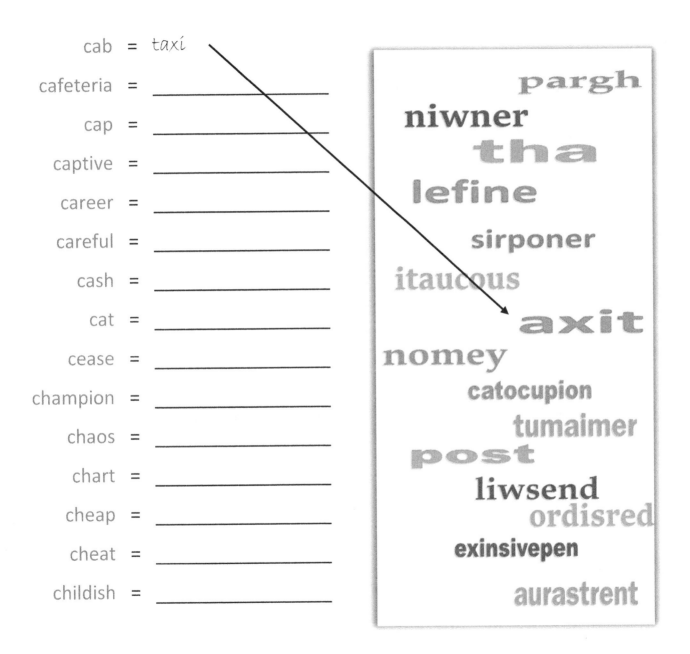

pargh

niwner

tha

lefine

sirponer

itaucous

axit

nomey

catocupion

tumaimer

post

liwsend

ordisred

exinsivepen

aurastrent

Pick One

Circle it, write it, explain your choice. You can only pick one. No cheating! This activity gets you thinking outside the box, and maybe, outside of your cell.

 Which is **warmer**, the handshake of a man who is guilty or the hug of a man who is not?

 Which is more **complete**, a letter you just started or the sentence you've just begun?

 Who is more **loved**, a guilty man who must serve many more years or an innocent man who gets to go home tonight?

 Who is more **missed**, the husband in jail or the wife at home?

 Who is **sadder**, the dad who sits behind bars or the child playing at the playground?

 Which is **blacker**, the vengeance a man promises to dish out or the punishment meted out by the judge?

 Which is **funnier**, the new fish who arrives with loudness or the old-timer who hasn't figured out how to live within the laws of the land?

Puzzlers

Ahhhh!
It's time for us to explore the
world of secret words,
confusing to those who can't
see beyond the letters and
numbers and symbols.
But you? You're smart.
So this will be a snap.
Easy. Simple.
Enjoy the challenge.
See if anyone else can
solve them...

bubububububububububu

walk

st RE ate

ever   ever

ever   ever

What words or phrases DO you see?

1. _____

2. _____

3. _____

4. _____

Think about it...

Suffering is simply a fact of our daily existence, as necessary to the process of growth and transformation as breath is to life.

And so, time passes, two days. It always does, not caring if we're happy or not. It passes.

-Sylvia Plath

Life is loneliness, despite the shrill tinsel of gaiety of "parties" with no purpose, despite the false grinning faces we all wear."

-Sylvia Plath

To live, or to die...

"I am but one more drop in the great sea of matter, defined, with the ability to realize my existences."

-Sylvia Plath

Making Words

How many words can you MAKE from these letters

A A I I C F G N N S T

SHORT words	MEDIUM words	LONG words
1-3 letters	4-6 letter word	7 or more letters

What is the 11-letter word that describes you? _____

Talking about...

Imagine that a **BUNK** could TALK. What would it **say**? Would it be **angry** or **happy** or **silly** or try to make a **joke** or **tease** or want to **play cards** or to be **alone**?

...to the **guy** who sleeps all day

_____
_____
_____

...to the **new guy** who put his dirty shoe on it

_____
_____
_____

...to the **coffee** that spilled on it

_____
_____
_____

...to the **nearest bunk**

_____
_____
_____

...to the **deputy** that tossed it

_____
_____
_____

Why do **you** want **to be free?**

List eight things you want to do on your first day of freedom.

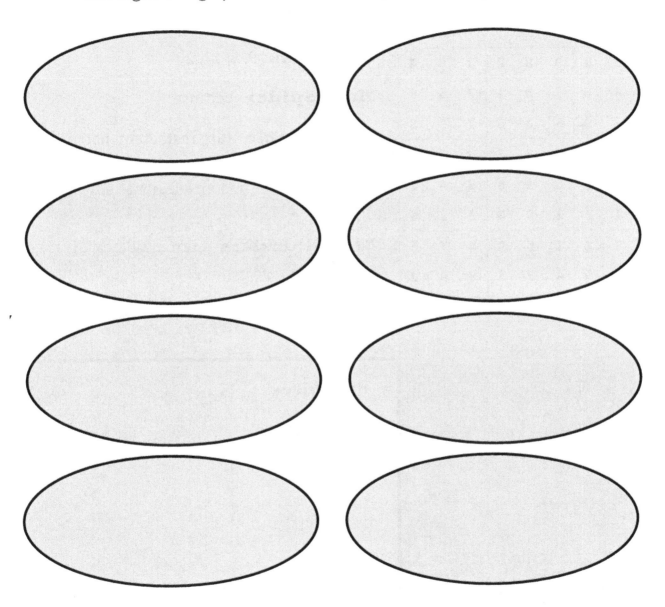

Answers

for Challenge THREE, cuz I already listed the answers for the first two sections, so I gotta do this one too.

3	5	1	9	8	2	7	6	4
4	8	6	7	3	1	2	5	9
2	7	9	5	4	6	1	3	8
6	4	8	3	5	7	9	2	1
9	2	3	6	1	8	5	4	7
5	1	7	2	9	4	3	8	6
8	3	2	1	6	9	4	7	5
1	6	5	4	7	3	8	9	2
7	9	4	8	2	5	6	1	3

Triangles: 9, 8, 12, 26

HangSpider: because

Unscramble: taxi, restaurant, hat, prisoner, occupation, cautious, money, feline, stop, winner, disorder, graph, inexpensive, swindle, immature

Word Puzzlers: button, sidewalk, reinstate, forever

Making Words: fascinating

> Be **anxious** for nothing, but in everything by **prayer** and **supplication**, with **thanksgiving**, let your requests be made known to God; and the **peace** of god, which surpasses all understanding, will guide your hearts and minds through Christ Jesus.

Philippians 4:6-7

Religion and Jesus-talk and prayer and Bible study is not just something that the accused does to look good in front of a judge. Your life and what you do is your choice. Be angry if you want, or vengeful or bitter. It's up to you. It's your mind and your emotions, your body and your life. But if you want peace, if you want a mind that is relaxed and can smile and laugh and fall asleep at night, then think about changing. Think about trying something else, because what you have been doing hasn't been working. It got you here, locked up, away from your family, away from the job and people and activities that are a part of a good life. If you want peace, then think about trying something else.

What things can you do today to bring peace to your mind?

Did you know...

1 Did you know that a roly-poly eats scat (poop) about one out of every ten meals?

2 Did you know that roly-polies live for 3-5 years?

3 Did you know that roly-polies are nocturnal, active at night, because they will dry up in the hot sun?

4 Did you know that some roly-polies have a chemical defense that will cause a wolf spider to sleep for twelve hours?

5 Did you know that roly-polies mate at night?

6 Did you know that a roly-poly can survive in a puddle by rolling into a ball?

7 Did you know that 12-100 babies will stay in their mother's pouch for 2-3 months until they are big enough to survive on their own?

	5			7			8	
1		3	5		9	7		2
	7		3	4	8		6	
	4	5		9		6	1	3
8		7	4		1	2		9
	9	1		5		8	7	
	1		9	8	4		2	
7	3	9	6		5	4		8
	2			1			9	

Yay! It's time for fun, that 1~2~3~4~5~6~7~8~9 game of Where does it go? and What goes here? and Ahhhhhh!

Enjoy yourself and don't let the numbers get you down.

He who tills his land will have **PLENTY** of **bread**, but he who *follows* frivolity will have **poverty** enough!
-Proverbs 28:19

Word Search

Here is another puzzle to do, with lots of hidden homonyms (same name) and homophones (same sound).

The words can be **horizontal, vertical, diagonal, forwards,** or **backwards.**

I filled up all the unused squares with the letter Z. Why this letter? I dunno. I just did.
Good luck!

W	E	D	O	R	D	E	R	Z	G	Z	Z	O	T	Z	F
Z	A	T	E	E	L	S	I	A	Z	H	T	H	G	I	E
E	S	V	D	A	E	R	T	F	E	L	Z	Z	R	K	E
V	I	D	E	E	R	E	Z	Y	Z	Y	D	E	E	N	B
A	G	E	X	A	C	T	W	O	N	Z	E	H	D	I	Z
R	H	O	N	E	S	Z	D	H	A	G	A	I	T	G	O
G	S	P	O	L	E	A	A	E	S	Y	R	Z	A	H	O
K	A	E	R	B	E	F	B	R	A	K	E	Z	E	T	T
G	R	O	W	N	Z	Z	A	Z	E	N	O	L	R	E	A
B	A	R	K	N	E	E	D	W	E	T	A	R	G	Z	B
P	T	W	O	L	O	A	N	Z	N	H	Z	E	L	I	P
E	R	I	G	H	T	N	A	O	R	G	Z	W	E	S	E
A	P	E	E	P	I	N	Z	W	R	I	T	E	Z	Z	A
K	U	Z	D	A	E	R	Z	E	Z	N	Z	T	Z	W	T
D	O	N	E	P	E	A	A	Z	Z	R	I	A	F	O	S
Z	I	Z	Y	E	N	E	E	D	E	L	S	I	O	N	U
K	Z	E	D	Z	Z	B	T	Z	P	I	R	T	S	K	J

Find these homonyms (words that are <u>spelled</u> alike but have two different <u>meanings</u>): bark, bat, bear, dear, down, exact, fair, fawn, fire, grave, just, kind, left, order, peak, pile, pole, trip, wave

Find these homophones (words that <u>sound</u> alike but are <u>spelled</u> differently): to, too, two, no, know, sighs, size, ate, eight, right, write, so, sew, due, dew, do, read, reed, need, knead, kneed, be, bee, die, dye, dear, deer, gait, gate, great, grate, night, knight, hey, hay, I, eye, aye, isle, aisle, pin, pen, pee, pea, see, sea, tee, tea, lone, loan, brake, break, grown, groan, one, won, owe, oh, red, read

Blah, blah, blah

How many **triangles** can **YOU** find?

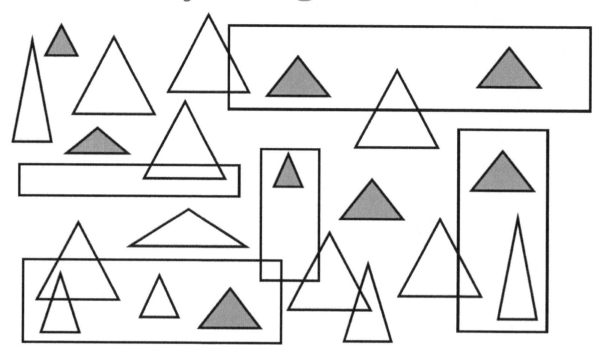

Hey, someone put **rectangles** in here. Yes, that was me. **Ignore** the rectangles unless they form a **triangle**. We're all about triangles here, so get to work:

1. How many shaded triangles do you see? ___

2. How many triangles touch another triangle? ___

3. How many triangles touch a rectangle's edge? ___

4. How many total triangles do you see? ___

Ten *action* **words** that describe JAIL

Think about action, things you do with your **hands** and **feet** and body, in the **morning**
and **afternoon** and **night**, when with one person and in a group.

1	6
2	7
3	8
4	9
5	10

One thing I like to do:

_____

_____

_____

_____

_____

I spot a butterfly on a flower. It is a gulf fritillary. Orange and black and white spots cover its wings. I watch it drink the nectar from the flower. Sweet. Satisfying. It clings to the florets and probes deep within with its proboscis, a tongue. I wonder if it remembers the time when it used to be a caterpillar, crawling everywhere it went, eating leaves but unable to fly. Can it remember, or is it stuck in the now, aware only of the present? I remember my past, long ago, when I was a child and dependent on others, wanting to make my own choices but forced to comply with my parents' rules and demands. I remember that time, long ago, when I was expected to be obedient and nice and thoughtful. I wonder how different I am today.

Don't hang the spider!

A = 3^2 x 2
B = 2^3 x 6
C = 7 x 5
D = 7 x 1
E = (3 x 3) x (5 + 2)
F = 5 x 2^2
G = (4 + 5) x (11 - 2)
H = 8 x 7
I = 7 x 6
J = 5^2 x 2^2
K = 6 x 5
L = 6 x 1
M = (3 + 4) x (2 + 2)
N = 3 x 3 x 3
O = 9 x (1 + 2 + 3 + 4)
P = 8 x 5
Q = 5^2
R = 9 x 1
S = 6 x 2
T = 1 + 2 + 3 + 4 + 5 + 6 + 7 + 8
U = (3 + 3 + 3) x (1 + 2 + 3)
V = 6 x 4
W = 7 x 3
X = 8 x 4
Y = (3 + 4) x (4 + 3)
Z = 4^3

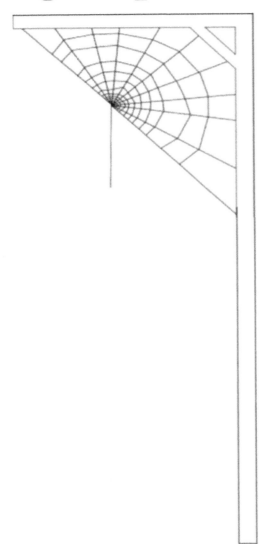

$\overline{20}$ $\overline{63}$ $\overline{48}$ $\overline{9}$ $\overline{54}$ $\overline{18}$ $\overline{9}$ $\overline{49}$

Watch a man and you will see his appetites.

– Confucius

Unscramble these WORDS

damage = *harm*

dampen = _____

daring = _____

dawn = _____

deadly = _____

deal = _____

deceive = _____

decide = _____

delicious = _____

delighted = _____

den = _____

depressed = _____

deserted = _____

desire = _____

destroy = _____

atalf
neomist
irtkc
selaped
shimedol
dobl
satty
dsa
shiw
rinusse
denonaband
rahm
rrubow
tenemegar
sohoce

Weird Facts about whatever...

In 2011, for no particular reason, 437 people dressed up as Superman. Could they fly or stop bullets? Nope.

1,436 people dressed as nuns in Ireland, guys too. Why? To raise money for a charity.

How long can you hold your breath? Well, don't try to set a world record because that belongs to Karoline Meyer of Brazil. In 2009 she held her breath underwater for 18 minutes. Yes, eighteen!

Who was the first person to do a 900 in competition? Tony Hawk, on his 11th attempt in Best Trick competition of the 1999 X-games.

Pick One

Circle it, write it, explain your choice. You can only pick one. No cheating! This activity gets you thinking outside the box, and maybe, outside of your cell.

 1. Which is **better**, a month in a loud dorm or a week in solitary?

 2. Which is **louder**, the words of a man's prayer or the actions of a silent man?

3. Which is more **blurry**, the steps you must take to gain your freedom or the memories you have of what it was like to be free?

 4. Which is more **likely**, that you'll learn to remain free once you're released or that you'll survive this stretch without a fight?

5. Which is more **painful**, apologizing to your family or thinking about the days ahead of you?

6. Which is less **real**, your memory of the event that got you here or the story you tell the guys locked up with you?

 7. Which is **slower**, the arrival of dinner on a hot summer day or awareness of your part in this fiasco?

WORD Puzzlers

Ahhhh!
It's time for us to explore the
world of secret words,
confusing to those who can't
see beyond the letters and
numbers and symbols.
But you? You're smart.
So this will be a snap.
Easy. Simple.
Enjoy the challenge.
See if anyone else can
solve them...

een   een
een   een
een   een
een   een

S
R
I
A
T
S

PANT ANT ANT PANT

10-S-E

What words or phrases DO YOU see?

1. _____

2. _____

3. _____

4. _____

Think about it...

> The difference between those who prevail and those who do not is the willingness to keep on.
>
> -Elizabeth Kaye

> Things happen,
>
> and they lead to
>
> other things.
>
> -Elizabeth Kaye

> You can have the talent for so many things and still be so daunted by the exertion they demand that you settle.
>
> -Elizabeth Kaye

> Things happen and they cannot be undone.
>
> -Elizabeth Kaye

> Change is so imperceptible as it occurs that only a backward glance can reveal its presence.
>
> -Elizabeth Kaye

Making Words

How many *words* can *you* MAKE from these letters

A E E U C F P L

SHORT words 1-3 letters	MEDIUM words 4-6 letter word	LONG words 7 or more letters

What is the 8-letter word that describes you? _____

Scribble, scribble...

Talking about...

Imagine that a **SANDAL** could TALK. What would it **say**? Would it be **angry** or **happy** or **silly** or try to make a **joke** or **tease** or want to **play cards** or to be **alone**?

...to the **stinky sock** stuck inside it

_____
_____
_____

...to the slimy **shower floor**

_____
_____
_____

...to the **toilet** it stands in front of

_____
_____
_____

...to the **guy** who stole it

_____
_____
_____

...to the **sandal** standing next to it

_____
_____
_____

What are my goals?

My goals for today are…	My goals for tomorrow are…
My goals for next year are…	My goals for ten years from now are…

Answers

for Challenge FOUR, cuz I know them and you need to know whether you're on the right track or not.

6	5	4	1	7	2	9	8	3
1	8	3	5	6	9	7	4	2
9	7	2	3	4	8	5	6	1
2	4	5	8	9	7	1	3	6
8	6	7	4	3	1	2	5	9
3	9	1	2	5	6	8	7	4
5	1	6	9	8	4	3	2	7
7	3	9	6	2	5	4	1	8
4	2	8	7	1	3	6	9	5

Triangles: 8, 4, 6, 29

HangSpider: February

Unscramble: harm, moisten, bold, sunrise, fatal, agreement, trick, choose, tasty, pleased, burrow, sad, abandoned, wish, demolish

Word Puzzlers: eighteen, upstairs, ants in your pants, Tennessee

Making Words: peaceful

Challenge FIVE

> But do not forget to DO **good** and to **share**, for with such sacrifices God is well pleased.

Hebrews 13:16

Sharing. We teach kids to share. Don't be selfish. Share with your little brother. And then we find ourselves grown-up and hairy and forget the things our parents taught us when we were first learning to speak. Look back on your life and think about the things your mom or dad, your grandma or grandpa taught you about how to treat others. Remember those words and ask yourself if you are doing what they taught you. Around you are a lot of sad guys. They may hide their emotions, masking them with bravado and bragging and bull-sh..., but underneath is a person who would love it if you shared what you have with them, a book, a pencil, a magazine, a deck of cards. You know what else you can share? Time. You have plenty of it.

What can you share, today, with the guy who seems to have lost hope?

Did you know...

1 Did you know that a worm will drown if there is too much rain, and that is why you find them on the sidewalk after a heavy rainstorm?

2 Did you know that worms have stiff bristles (hairs) on each segment that grip the earth when they wiggle through the soil?

3 Did you know that a worm's skin can sense the light and taste their food?

4 Did you know that worms are both male and female (they are hermaphrodites)?

5 Did you know that the longest worms are in Australia and Asia and can reach a length of thirteen feet?

6 Did you know that an earthworm can feel the vibrations of a bird hopping on the ground above?

7 Did you know that an acre of land can have up to one million worms?

Sudoku

		6	4		5	3		
5		2				4		7
7		3	2	6	8	5		1
2	6	4				8	1	3
		5		4		6		
9	7	8				2	5	4
4		7	9	8	6	1		5
8		9				7		6
		1	7		3	9		

Yay! It's time for fun, that
1-2-3-4-5-6-7-8-9 game of
Where does it go? and
What goes here? and
Ahhhhhh!

Enjoy yourself and don't
let the numbers get you
down.

The **way** of a fool is **right** in his *own eyes*:
but he who heeds **COUNSEL** is wise.

-Proverbs 12:15

Word Search

Three-letter words.
This puzzle is full of them.

They can be **horizontal**,
vertical, **diagonal**,
forwards, or **backwards**.

Can you find them?
The list is down below.

Have fun.

O	I	L	P	I	K	S	B	I	T	U	N	O	W	O	V
P	A	D	A	X	I	F	E	W	A	H	A	M	A	O	A
O	T	A	N	R	A	N	D	Z	F	A	N	A	J	E	T
T	G	Y	K	D	K	A	Y	A	O	D	O	J	A	B	Q
T	E	A	I	T	W	O	P	P	R	K	A	O	R	O	U
A	L	L	P	O	U	S	E	M	A	Y	R	B	D	O	O
T	C	A	I	P	H	O	W	U	F	P	A	E	S	D	S
U	L	W	B	P	I	M	U	G	I	E	E	B	A	E	A
M	A	D	Y	E	T	E	G	A	N	T	E	G	G	I	Y
E	A	R	O	F	F	P	A	G	O	U	L	L	I	C	R
N	D	A	Y	N	A	V	S	T	Y	P	K	A	D	O	T
D	A	C	O	P	E	E	V	I	A	B	A	G	U	B	A
A	M	A	N	Y	X	T	V	K	N	I	C	Y	H	A	S
W	A	B	R	U	G	A	T	E	W	C	R	Y	R	D	A
K	Y	N	E	W	P	W	W	T	Y	E	H	W	K	I	D
S	A	A	I	I	A	A	I	T	E	M	A	P	E	O	F
A	R	M	Z	X	R	Y	G	A	R	N	T	O	Y	B	I

Find these words: act, air, and, ant, any, all, ape, arm, ask, bad, bag, bee, beg, bug, bit, boo, cab, cop,, car, cut, cob, cry, day, dam dry, dot, dig, ear, egg, elk, emu, end, eve, fan, fat, few, fin, fir, fix, for, gag, gap, gas, get, gum, had, ham, has, hat, hey, hit, how, ice, ill, ink, icy, irk, jab, jam ,jar, jaw, jet, job, key, kid, koi, kit, lab, lag, lap, law, lay, leg, let, lid, lip, mad, man, map, may, met, net, new, nix, nod, nut, oak, oar, odd, off, oil, one, pad, pan, pay, pet, pot, put, quo, rag, rap, ray, rug, sad, sag, sat, say, sea, spa, ski, tea, top, try, two, tan, tow, toy, use, ump, van, vat vet, via, vie, vow, wad, war wax, way, web, wet, wig, won, yak, yam, yet, yon, yes, zap, zip

Oops!

How many **triangles** can YOU find?

Hey, someone put **pentagons** in here. Yes, that was me, again. **Ignore** these five-sided polygons unless they form a **triangle**. We're all about triangles here, so get to work:

1. How many shaded triangles do you see? ____

2. How many triangles touch another triangle? ____

3. How many triangles touch a pentagon's edge? ____

4. How many total triangles do you see? ____

Ten *shapely* **words** that describe ME

Think about what makes you YOU, the things people **see** and **hear**, the **action** and **words** that come from you, alone and with others.

Round

Square

Straight

Curvy

Connected

Soft

Hard

My best quality: _____

_____

_____

_____

_____

A squirrel jumps from the trail onto an oak tree as I approach. He stares at me and chatters his annoyance, bothered that I interrupted his afternoon hunt. I apologize, and watch him scamper away, but is it really my fault. I came out here because I wanted to see wildlife. I chose to be here. Should I feel guilty over being where I want to be? I shake my head and tell him so. This is my world too. Share it with me. I have a life to live, fun times I want to experience, laughter and excitement and new things. I won't apologize for wanting to get everything I can out of life. I only get one chance to live today, and then it is gone. Tomorrow might be full of rainclouds and coldness, confining me indoors. Today I had a chance to be out here, so I came.

Don't hang the spider!

$A = 3^2 \times 2$

$B = 2^3 \times 6$

$C = 7 \times 5$

$D = 7 \times 1$

$E = (3 \times 3) \times (5 + 2)$

$F = 5 \times 2^2$

$G = (4 + 5) \times (11 - 2)$

$H = 8 \times 7$

$I = 7 \times 6$

$J = 5^2 \times 2^2$

$K = 6 \times 5$

$L = 6 \times 1$

$M = (3 + 4) \times (2 + 2)$

$N = 3 \times 3 \times 3$

$O = 9 \times (1 + 2 + 3 + 4)$

$P = 8 \times 5$

$Q = 5^2$

$R = 9 \times 1$

$S = 6 \times 2$

$T = 1 + 2 + 3 + 4 + 5 + 6 + 7 + 8$

$U = (3 + 3 + 3) \times (1 + 2 + 3)$

$V = 6 \times 4$

$W = 7 \times 3$

$X = 8 \times 4$

$Y = (3 + 4) \times (4 + 3)$

$Z = 4^3$

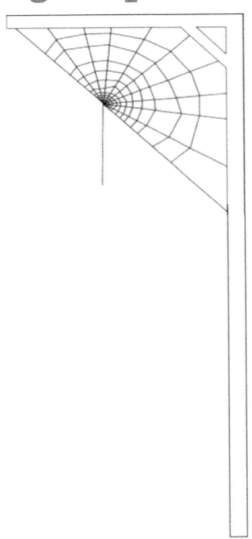

$\overline{20}$ $\overline{63}$ $\overline{48}$ $\overline{9}$ $\overline{54}$ $\overline{18}$ $\overline{9}$ $\overline{49}$

Don't **be** ashamed to admit your faults.

– Confucius

Unscramble these WORDS

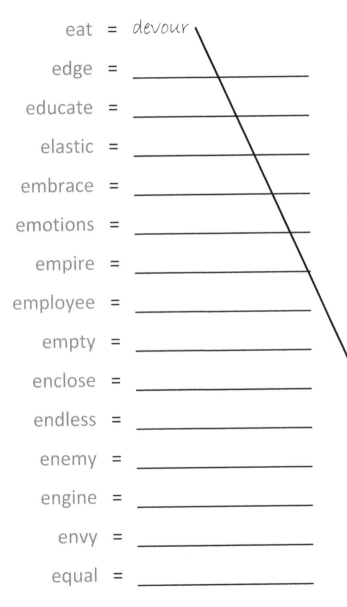

eat = *devour*

edge = _____

educate = _____

elastic = _____

embrace = _____

emotions = _____

empire = _____

employee = _____

empty = _____

enclose = _____

endless = _____

enemy = _____

engine = _____

envy = _____

equal = _____

ugh

ginkmod

arsyvader

rowerk

cheat

rusnourd

saulejoy

cintedial

tertschy

dietlunim

vedour

cavtan

leefsing

tromo

roberd

Pick One

Circle it, write it, explain your choice. You can only pick one. No cheating! This activity gets you thinking outside the box, and maybe, outside of your cell.

 Which is **hotter**, your temper at an annoying inmate or the nurse who delivers meds**?**

Which more **harmful**, the drugs you traded to another guy or the words you spoke about the deputy**?**

 Which is more **meaningful**, to read the Bible each day or to ask for forgiveness from those you hurt**?**

Which is less **wasteful**, to give your unwanted food to the homeless guy or to make a list of what you want to do when you get out**?**

 Which is more **memorable**, your last meal on the outside or how you felt that first night locked up**?**

Which is more **aggravating**, the story you have to listen to again and again or the limited floor space you walk over every day**?**

 Who is more **thankful**, the man who gets visits each week or the visitor who hears "I will be out soon" **?**

WORD Puzzlers

Ahhhh!
It's time for us to explore the
world of secret words,
confusing to those who can't
see beyond the letters and
numbers and symbols.
But you? You're smart.
So this will be a snap.
Easy. Simple.
Enjoy the challenge.
See if anyone else can
solve them...

4est

 wolf

angle

ar*arm*m

What words or phrases DO you see?

1. _____   2. _____

3. _____   4. _____

Think about it...

Certain things seem so crucial at the time, yet ultimately make no difference.

-Elizabeth Kaye

I wanted what a person often wants when they're confined to a bed for most of the day, which is a moment of contact with another human soul.

-Elizabeth Kaye

Life does not afford the time to do it all.

-Elizabeth Kaye

It is possible to walk with bloody feet.

-Elizabeth Kaye

The most difficult aspect...was being left behind, seeing oneself ignored by people who once would have gone to lengths to be ingratiating.

-Elizabeth Kaye

Making Words

How many words can you MAKE from these letters

A E I I U C H N S S T T

SHORT words	MEDIUM words	LONG words
1-3 letters	4-6 letter word	7 or more letters

What is the 12-letter word that describes you? _____

Grab a pencil and write SOMETHING positive about yourself!

_____

_____

_____

_____

_____

_____

_____

_____

_____

_____

_____

Weird Facts *about* **whatever...**

McDonalds
is in
119 countries.

Coca-Cola began
making soda in
1886.

Anything
we do
alters the brain.

-Scientific American

Neurons in the brain's reward system squirt out a chemical messenger called dopamine, giving us a little wave of satisfaction. But give yourself a lot and the brain squirts out less and feels the high only with more.

How to solve a problem

1st identify the problem
2nd analyze the problem
3rd think of alternatives
4th apply previous knowledge
5th make a decision

What are four common **PROBLEMS** that you face in jail?

Answers

for Challenge FIVE cuz it's the end of the book now and you're expecting it.

1	9	6	4	7	5	3	8	2
5	8	2	3	1	9	4	6	7
7	4	3	2	6	8	5	9	1
2	6	4	5	9	7	8	1	3
3	1	5	8	4	2	6	7	9
9	7	8	6	3	1	2	5	4
4	3	7	9	8	6	1	2	5
8	2	9	1	5	4	7	3	6
6	5	1	7	2	3	9	4	8

Triangles: 12, 4, 5, 30

HangSpider: practically

Unscramble: devour, border, teach, stretchy, hug, feelings, kingdom, worker, vacant, surround, unlimited, adversary, motor, jealousy, identical

Word Puzzlers: forest, big bad wolf, right angle, arm in arm

Pattern: xxxx

Making Words: enthusiastic

Improve yourself

while in jail or prison

ANOTHER of my **Books**

you *might* **want** to **check out**...

Anger Management
Jail/Prison Bible Study Series, vol. 1

What are your PLANS for when you finish serving your sentence in jail/prison, and you are free to go where you want?

Where is your SAFE PLACE to calm down and get back in control of your emotions after you are angered?

Describe two moments today when you were **calm** inside even though there was annoying noise or chaos all around you.

Is there a difference between what you FEEL on the inside and what you DO on the outside?

Tell about a moment in jail/ prison that involved someone's anger directed at you.

ANOTHER of my **Books**

you *might* **want** to **check out**...

Other Jail/Prison books you might be interested in:

If someone in your family is ordering this for you, remind them to purchase a new copy from Amazon (most county jails and state prisons will not accept books from an outside vendor). All my books are available through Amazon, just search for "C. Mahoney" and the title. Or, search for "Mahoney jail or prison".

Keeping the Mind Active in Jail or Prison - Hidden Secrets
Keeping the Mind Active in Jail or Prison - Optical Illusions
Keeping the Mind Active in Jail or Prison - Visual Puzzles

Anger Management (**Jail/Prison Bible Study Series**, Vol 1)
Finding Happiness (**Jail/Prison Bible Study Series**, Vol 2)
Learning to Listen (**Jail/Prison Bible Study Series**, Vol 3)
Patiently Waiting (**Jail/Prison Bible Study Series**, Vol 4)
Peaceful Respect (**Jail/Prison Bible Study Series**, Vol 5)
Kindness to Others (**Jail/Prison Bible Study Series**, Vol 6)

Surviving the Stress: a gift for a loved one in jail or prison
Surviving the Insanity: a gift for a loved one in jail or prison
Doing More Than Survive: a gift for a loved one in jail or prison

75 Fun Facts to Help you Beat the Boredom of Jail or Prison
75 Interesting Facts to Help you Beat the Boredom of Jail or Prison
75 Strange Facts to Help you Beat the Boredom of Jail or Prison
75 Weird Facts to Help you Beat the Boredom of Jail or Prison
250 Things to Write about...in jail
Become a Better Writer in Jail or Prison
Encouraging Words for someone in Jail or Prison
Improve yourself while in Jail or prison
Making Choices - A book of Moral Dilemmas for Someone in Jail or Prison

Psalm 119 - A Study Guide for Someone in Jail or Prison
Questions for Someone in Jail or Prison
Sudoku for the Guy in Jail or Prison
Surviving Jail or Prison - Creative Writing to Help You Grow
Surviving Jail or Prison - Making Better Choices
Surviving Jail or Prison - Questions to Think About
Surviving Jail or Prison - Thinking About my Life
Thinking and Writing while in Jail or Prison - Exploring African Wisdom
Thinking and Writing while in Jail or Prison - Exploring Buddhist Wisdom
Thinking and Writing while in Jail or Prison - Exploring Native American Wisdom
Thinking and Writing while in Jail or Prison - Exploring The Wisdom of Confucius
Thinking and Writing while in Jail or Prison - Exploring the Wisdom of Gandhi
Thinking and Writing while in Jail or Prison - Exploring Unitarian Universalist Wisdom
Thinking and Writing while in Jail or Prison - Exploring Zoroastrian Wisdom
Word Puzzles to keep the mind sharp in Jail

Wildlife Bible (This is a very cool collection 250 Bible verses and 250 wildlife photos that I took...250 pages that you won't find anywhere else.)

Made in United States
Orlando, FL
29 April 2022